MONSTER MADNESS

THE STORY OF ZOMBIES

JENNIFER LOMBARDO

Please visit our website, www.enslow.com. For a free color catalog of all our high-quality books, call toll free 1-800-398-2504 or fax 1-877-980-4454.

Library of Congress Cataloging-in-Publication Data
Names: Lombardo, Jennifer, author.
Title: The story of zombies / by Jennifer Lombardo.
Description: New York : Enslow Publishing, 2023. | Series: Monster madness | Includes index.
Identifiers: LCCN 2022001173 | ISBN 9781978531864 (library binding) | ISBN 9781978531840 (paperback) | ISBN 9781978531857 (set) | ISBN 9781978531871 (ebook)
Subjects: LCSH: Zombies–Juvenile literature.
Classification: LCC GR581 .L66 2023 | DDC 398.21–dc23/eng/20220126
LC record available at https://lccn.loc.gov/2022001173

Published in 2023 by
Enslow Publishing
29 E. 21st Street
New York, NY 10010

Copyright © 2023 Enslow Publishing

Designer: Tanya Dellaccio
Editor: Jennifer Lombardo

Photo credits: Cover Memo Angeles/Shutterstock.com; p. 5 (top) Nebojsa Markovic/Shutterstock.com; p. 5 (bottom) kotyache/Shutterstock.com; p. 7 https://commons.wikimedia.org/wiki/File:Frontispiece_from_the_book_Saint-Domingue,_ou_Histoire_de_Ses_R%C3%A9volutions._ca._1815.jpg; p. 9 (top) benoitb/iStock Images; p. 7 (bottom) https://commons.wikimedia.org/wiki/File:MarieLaveau_(Frank_Schneider).png; p. 11 https://commons.wikimedia.org/wiki/File:WhiteZombieBelaLugosiCrop.png; p. 13 (bottom) TCD/Prod.DB/Alamy Images; p. 13 (top) Photo 12/Alamy Images; p. 15 Osvaldo Olmos/Shutterstock.com; p. 17 Moviestore Collection Ltd/Alamy Images; p. 19 (both) val lawless/Shutterstock.com; p. 21 Christina Kennedy/Alamy Images.

All rights reserved. No part of this book may be reproduced in any form without permission in writing from the publisher, except by a reviewer.

Printed in the United States of America

Some of the images in this book illustrate individuals who are models. The depictions do not imply actual situations or events.

CPSIA compliance information: Batch #CSENS23: For further information contact Enslow Publishing, New York, New York, at 1-800-398-2504.

CONTENTS

WHAT'S A ZOMBIE? 4

THE FIRST ZOMBIES 6

THE FIRST ZOMBIE MOVIE 10

THE WAY WE SEE ZOMBIES 12

BRAINS! 14

FAST OR SLOW? 16

FROM A MISTAKE 18

MAKE A PLAN! 20

GLOSSARY 22

FOR MORE INFORMATION 23

INDEX 24

Boldface words appear in the glossary.

WHAT'S A ZOMBIE?

Zombies are a **category** of creature called the undead. This means they aren't really alive, but they aren't exactly dead either. Vampires, skeletons, and mummies are other examples of undead monsters.

Zombies are undead because they're people who have been **reanimated** after they died. In most zombie stories, they come back to life because of a virus. This virus makes them forget who they used to be. It also makes them want to eat people! When they bite someone, they give them the virus. This is how more zombies are made.

MANY PEOPLE LIKE TO DRESS UP AS ZOMBIES FOR HALLOWEEN, PARADES, AND PARTIES!

BELIEVE IT OR NOT!

BECAUSE ZOMBIES ARE UNDEAD, THINGS THAT WOULD KILL A LIVING PERSON DON'T USUALLY HURT THEM. MOST PEOPLE AGREE THAT THE ONLY WAY TO MAKE SURE A ZOMBIE STAYS DEAD IS TO DESTROY THEIR BRAIN IN SOME WAY.

THE FIRST ZOMBIES

From the 1600s to the 1800s, France kidnapped people from Africa and enslaved them in Haiti. France controlled Haiti at the time.

These enslaved people suffered a lot. They believed that if they died of illness or old age, their souls would go back to Africa. If they died in any other way, the enslaved people believed they would have to stay on the **plantations** in Haiti forever. They would never be able to rest or go home.

THIS PICTURE SHOWS ENSLAVED HAITIANS FIGHTING FOR THEIR FREEDOM IN 1791.

The zombie **myth** changed a little after Haiti won its **independence** from France in 1804. People who followed the Haitian religion of voodoo believed a dead person could be brought back to life by a *bokor*, or a person who could do magic. The zombie would have to do anything the *bokor* wanted.

Today, people are scared that zombies will hurt them. However, Haitians at this time were scared of becoming zombies and not being able to make their own choices. It would be like being enslaved again after death.

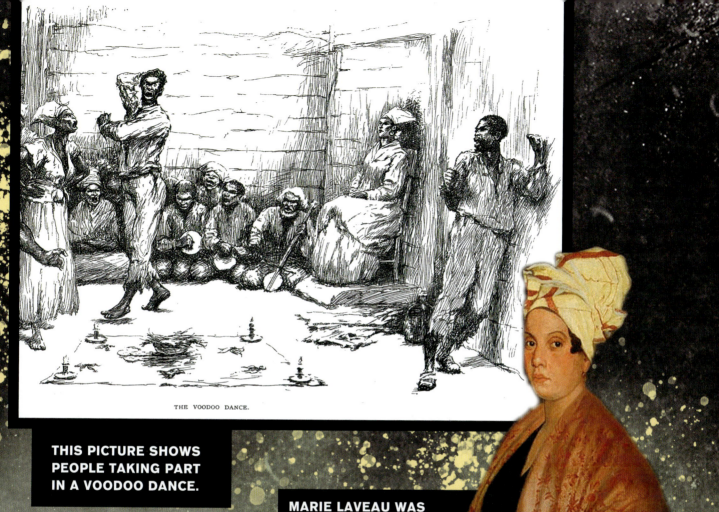

THE VOODOO DANCE.

THIS PICTURE SHOWS PEOPLE TAKING PART IN A VOODOO DANCE.

MARIE LAVEAU WAS A FAMOUS VOODOO PRIESTESS IN NEW ORLEANS, LOUISIANA.

BELIEVE IT OR NOT!

UNTIL 1803, FRANCE ALSO CONTROLLED THE PART OF NORTH AMERICA THAT IS NOW THE STATE OF LOUISIANA. A LOT OF HAITIANS MOVED THERE BETWEEN 1790 AND 1809. THEY BROUGHT VOODOO AND THEIR BELIEF IN ZOMBIES WITH THEM.

THE FIRST ZOMBIE MOVIE

Zombie movies have become very popular over the years. The first one was called *White Zombie*. It came out in 1932. It told the story of a Haitian plantation owner who fell in love with a woman who was marrying another man. He asked a *bokor* to turn her into a zombie so she would marry him instead.

Not many people liked *White Zombie* when it first came out. In 1968, a much more popular movie called *Night of the Living Dead* came out. It was directed by George A. Romero.

THIS PICTURE IS FROM *WHITE ZOMBIE*.

BELIEVE IT OR NOT!

IN *NIGHT OF THE LIVING DEAD*, NO ONE USES THE WORD "ZOMBIE." INSTEAD, THEY CALL THEM GHOULS. ROMERO SAID A FRENCH MOVIE MAGAZINE WAS THE FIRST TO CALL THEM ZOMBIES, AND THE NAME STUCK!

THE WAY WE SEE ZOMBIES

Night of the Living Dead gave us a lot of our ideas about how zombies look and act. The zombies in the movie walked slowly. They didn't talk, but they did groan. They were the first zombies to be made undead by a virus and to want to eat people.

The movie was also the first to show a lot of people turned into zombies at once. It showed how hard it would be to fight them, especially if people didn't work together. This is where we get the idea of a zombie **apocalypse**.

ROMERO GOT MANY OF HIS IDEAS FROM BOOKS AND COMIC BOOKS.

BELIEVE IT OR NOT!

FOR MANY YEARS AFTER THE MOVIE CAME OUT, PEOPLE USED ROMERO'S EXACT IDEAS OF WHAT ZOMBIES WERE LIKE FOR THEIR OWN MOVIES AND ZOMBIE STORIES.

13

BRAINS!

In 1985, a director named Dan O'Bannon made a movie called *Return of the Living Dead*. In this movie, the zombies can talk, but not very well. The only thing they really say is, "Brains!" This movie is the one that gave us the idea that zombies want to eat our brains. In Romero's movies, the zombies will eat any part of the body.

This movie wasn't very popular, so the only part of it that changed the way we see zombies was the part about brains. Today, the **classic** idea of a zombie is a Romero-style zombie that eats brains.

ZOMBIE COSTUMES OFTEN INCLUDE BRAINS IN SOME WAY.

BELIEVE IT OR NOT!

WHEN FANS MET ROMERO, THEY WOULD OFTEN ASK HIM TO SIGN SOMETHING WITH "EAT BRAINS!" ROMERO ONCE SAID HE WAS CONFUSED BY THIS, SINCE NONE OF THE ZOMBIES IN HIS MOVIES EAT BRAINS. HE DIDN'T KNOW WHERE THAT CAME FROM!

FAST OR SLOW?

Over time, people started making changes to zombies in stories and movies. Some people made their zombies move quickly. They could run and climb, which made them harder to get away from and harder to kill. You have to move quickly to beat a fast zombie!

Some people think fast zombies are scarier. Others say slow zombies are. A slow zombie is easier to run from, but it never stops coming, so it can outlast a person. A large group of slow zombies can also **overwhelm** a person or group of people.

FAST AND SLOW ZOMBIE MOVIES

FAST	SLOW
28 DAYS LATER	DAWN OF THE DEAD (1978)
ARMY OF THE DEAD	DAY OF THE DEAD
DAWN OF THE DEAD (2004)	LITTLE MONSTERS
I AM LEGEND	NIGHT OF THE LIVING DEAD
RESIDENT EVIL	PLANET TERROR
TRAIN TO BUSAN	SHAUN OF THE DEAD
WORLD WAR Z	WARM BODIES

WHICH DO YOU THINK IS SCARIER: FAST OR SLOW ZOMBIES?

BELIEVE IT OR NOT!

ZOMBIES AREN'T JUST FOR THE MOVIES! THEY'RE IN VIDEO GAMES SUCH AS *MINECRAFT* AND *PLANTS VS. ZOMBIES*. THEY'RE IN MICHAEL JACKSON'S 1983 "THRILLER" MUSIC VIDEO. THEY'RE IN HUNDREDS OF BOOKS, INCLUDING COMIC BOOKS. THERE ARE ZOMBIE GAMES, COSTUMES, AND MORE!

MICHAEL JACKSON'S "THRILLER" VIDEO

FROM A MISTAKE

When people invent things—including movies and books—they often copyright them. This means the person who invented the thing is the only one who gets to decide how it gets used.

When *Night of the Living Dead* came out, someone forgot to put the copyright **symbol** next to the movie's title. The law at the time said that meant it wasn't copyrighted! Because of that, anyone could use Romero's zombies. If the movie had been copyrighted correctly, we wouldn't have all the zombie things that we do today!

BELIEVE IT OR NOT!

A 5K IS A RACE THAT'S 5 KILOMETERS (3.1 MILES) LONG. THERE ARE SOME 5KS WHERE PEOPLE ARE CHASED BY ZOMBIES AS THEY RUN! MOST OF THESE RACES ALSO HAVE MUD PITS, CLIMBING WALLS, AND OTHER **OBSTACLES** FOR THE RUNNERS.

SOME RACERS DRESS UP WHEN THEY RUN A ZOMBIE 5K.

MAKE A PLAN!

Some people find it fun to think about how they'd live through the zombie apocalypse. These people carefully plan where they'd hide, what weapons they'd use, how they'd get food, and much more.

One of the most famous zombie books is *The Zombie Survival Guide* by Max Brooks. It gives people information about classic zombies to help them with their plans. It also gives people ideas about what kinds of supplies they might need, how to guard their home, and the best ways to kill zombies.

WHAT'S YOUR ZOMBIE APOCALYPSE PLAN?

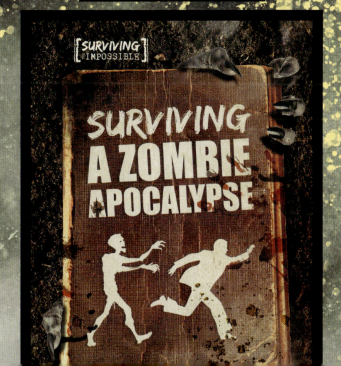

GLOSSARY

apocalypse: A great disaster.

category: Class or group.

classic: Being typical of its kind.

independence: The state of being independent, or free from outside control.

myth: A legend or story.

obstacle: Something that blocks a path.

overwhelm: To overcome completely.

plantations: Large farms.

reanimate: To give new life or energy to something.

symbol: A picture, shape, or object that stands for something else.

FOR MORE INFORMATION

BOOKS

Cole, Bradley. *Zombies.* Oxford, UK: Raintree, 2021.

Moon, Walt K. *Zombies.* San Diego, CA: BrightPoint Press, 2022.

Ogden, Charlie. *Surviving a Zombie Apocalypse.* New York, NY: Gareth Stevens Publishing, 2018

WEBSITES

Britannica Kids: "Zombie"
kids.britannica.com/kids/article/zombie/600661
Learn more about the history of zombies.

Novel Games: Cure the Zombies
www.novelgames.com/en/curethezombies
Try to save the world from zombies in this fun spelling game.

Science News for Students: "Zombies Are Real!"
www.sciencenewsforstudents.org/article/zombies-are-real
Read about zombies in nature.

Publisher's note to educators and parents: Our editors have carefully reviewed these websites to ensure that they are suitable for students. Many websites change frequently, however, and we cannot guarantee that a site's future contents will continue to meet our high standards of quality and educational value. Be advised that students should be closely supervised whenever they access the internet.

INDEX

bokor, 10, 8

brains, 5, 14, 15

copyright, 18

5K race, 19

Haiti, 6, 7, 8, 9, 10

Night of the Living Dead, 10, 11, 12, 17, 18

Return of the Living Dead, 14

Romero, George A., 10, 11, 12, 13, 14, 15, 18

slavery, 6, 7, 8

undead, 4, 5, 12

virus, 4, 12

White Zombie, 10, 11

zombie apocalypse, 12, 20, 21

Zombie Survival Guide, The, 20